D1518476

Choosing a Career in the Fashion Industry

John Giacobello

Jobs in the fashion industry range from high-profile to low key.

Choosing a Career in the Fashion Industry

John Giacobello

The Rosen Publishing Group, Inc.
New York

Published in 2000 by The Rosen Publishing Group, Inc.
29 East 21st Street, New York, NY 10010

Library of Congress Cataloging-in-Publication Data

Giacobello, John.
Careers in the fashion industry / John Giacobello
    p. cm.—(World of work)
Includes bibliographical references (p.) and index.
Summary: Provides information about the fashion industry, common careers in fashion, and how to prepare for them.
    ISBN 0-8239-3296-6 (lib. bdg.)
  1. Fashion—Vocational guidance—Juvenile literature. 2. Clothing trade—Vocational guidance—Juvenile literature. [1. Fashion—Vocational guidance. 2. Clothing trade—Vocational guidance. 3. Vocational guidance.] I. Title. II. World of work (New York, N.Y.)
TT507.G4823 2000
746.92'023—dc21

00-008291

Manufactured in the United States of America

Contents

Introduction

*I*n the eleventh grade, Tabitha started to think about career options. When she told her parents she was interested in fashion, they shook their heads. "Better think of something else, sweetie," her father said. "Fashion is hard to get into."

Her mother agreed. "Shauna Jones's daughter went to school for fashion," she said. "Now she can barely support herself because her new job pays so little."

Tabitha was disappointed. She loved reading fashion magazines and had a great sense of style. She also loved to sew and take photographs. Since talking to her parents had made her feel discouraged, Tabitha decided to go to her school counselor, Mr. Riince. He explained that while some fashion jobs can be low paying and difficult to get into, the pay usually increases with time and experience. He also pointed out that stiff competition should not discourage a person from *doing what he or she really wants to do and that there are other fashion jobs with higher entry-level pay, less intense competition, and high job security.*

Tabitha started feeling happier. She still was not sure what kind of fashion job she was looking for. But at least she realized that working in fashion was not an impossible dream.

Jobs in the fashion industry do have a reputation for being unstable, low paying, and competitive. However, for those who are willing to accept these negative aspects, there are plenty of good things that make up for the occasional hassle or two. Many models, designers, and photographers choose and enjoy being a part of these less predictable careers because they thrive in this kind of less rigid and more creative atmosphere.

For those who seek a more secure career path with fewer surprises, many lesser-known fashion jobs offer job security and higher entry-level pay. The jobs described in chapter 3 tend to be more of a sure bet as far as a steady paycheck is concerned.

The important thing is not to be put off by fashion's bad rap. There are exciting jobs in this field for everyone. While you read through this book, think about the kind of person you are and how your personality traits might be best matched to some of the careers listed. Whatever your talents or interests, remember to keep an open mind as you explore the many sides of fashion.

Window display designers use their visual creativity to help sell clothes.

The World of Fashion

When you pick up the latest issue of *Vogue* or catch a glamorous runway show on television, you may wonder what the world of fashion is really like. You might even wish you could be part of it. A fashion career can bring you closer to the lights, the models, the guest list, and all of the excitement you dream about. A career in fashion can also take you behind the scenes, far from the flash-bulbs and fanfare. Jobs in this industry range from high profile—being a model or designer—to low key—being a photographer's assistant or ware-house inventory manager or a copy editor at a fashion magazine.

The word "fashion" might bring to mind vis-ions of Naomi Campbell or Cindy Crawford in bright feathers and lace, or designer Isaac Mizrahi backstage gluing sequins on a gown. Some might think of a glossy magazine spread shot by a famous photographer. However, most people do not realize how many different kinds of people help to keep the wheels of fashion spinning.

For example, window display designers help

to sell clothing by creating exciting displays for department store windows. Makeup artists and cosmetologists help both models and fashion consumers look their best. Without seamstresses and tailors, many great outfits would not fit properly. And those who work in fashion retailing—everyone from cashier to manager, buyer, and sales representative—provide an essential link between fashion and its customers. And these are just a few examples of lesser-known fashion careers!

The Business of Fashion

Fashion is an important industry that touches most people's lives in some way. The clothing industry blossomed a little over 100 years ago when sewing machines became powerful enough to manufacture garments on a large scale. Clothing factories popped up all over the United States, especially in New York City. To this day, New York City remains an important fashion center for the entire world.

As the clothing industry developed, very wealthy people were able to have elegant garments designed just for them. Other designers would copy these styles, re-create them using inexpensive fabrics, and sell them at low prices. This allowed the middle classes to purchase "designer" clothing. Everyone else kept up with the styles of the rich by reading fashion magazines. This is how the current fashion industry came into being.

Today, fashion works in much the same way.

The clothing industry started a little over 100 years ago, with the introduction of sewing machines powerful enough to manufacture garments on a large scale.

Very few people can afford the clothes that are paraded on the runway. But those high fashion designs influence the less expensive items you see when you shop at a department store. And magazines still provide inspiration for men and women from all walks of life.

Fashion Personalities

It is difficult to define one specific personality type that fits into the fashion world. This is because there are many different parts of the fashion industry. For example, someone who is extremely organized and seeks high job security would be an excellent candidate for a career in department store management. Those with fashion foresight and artistic skills might make a great designer or photographer. An assertive individual who enjoys working with people could do well as a sales representative.

To help you figure out what your place in the fashion world may be, here are some good questions to ask yourself:

✔ **Do you believe in fashion?**
This might seem like a simple question, but the fashion industry sometimes brings out mixed emotions or negative feelings in people. Some people feel that fashion television shows and magazines exploit women by reducing them to objects. Many feminists are against fashion because they believe that it forces women to dress uncomfortably in order to please men. It has also been said that the overly thin body types presented in the fashion world contribute to low self-esteem and eating disorders among young women and men.

These are opinions and are not necessarily true or untrue. Many people find fashion empowering and say that dressing fashionably makes them feel good about themselves, while giving them an outlet to express their creativity and sense of style. Others suggest that there is no real evidence of a connection between the frenzy over superthin models and eating disorders. These are important issues to consider before deciding on a fashion career. You and only you can decide what you believe.

✔ **Do you like to work with a variety of personalities?**
The fashion industry is filled with many different types of people. Regardless of whether you cut patterns, model, or design bridal gowns, you will meet many interesting personalities. Because of this, it is especially important that you are able to effectively communicate with people from all walks of life. This is true in any industry, but the fashion industry in particular has a reputation for attracting a variety of sometimes eccentric minds. An accepting and flexible attitude is an important asset in the fashion world.

✔ **What do you do with your free time?**
Think about the kinds of activities or interests that you engage in that might pertain to your future career. What kinds of part-time jobs have you had, if any? What do you do in your spare time? Make a list of your hobbies, activities, and accomplishments. Now try to decide what these things say about you. If you enjoy acting or going to plays, perhaps designing costumes for the theater would be an interesting career possibility to explore. If you have worked as a cashier at a grocery store, your retail experience could be translated into a fashion-retailing career. If you are a fan of MTV, you may be interested in image making and marketing.

✔ **Which classes do you most enjoy?**
Do you prefer art class or math? Does studying human anatomy interest you, or is English

your specialty? Knowing which classes you enjoy and excel at can help you determine what direction you should travel within or outside of the fashion industry.

Keep these questions in mind as you read the following chapters. A career in the fashion industry is not for everyone, and the best way to find out if this is a good choice for you is to be aware of the types of fashion careers that exist in and out of the spotlight.

The Art and Craft of Fashion

The fashion industry offers many opportunities for creative expression. If you are artistic or are skilled with your hands, there are terrific possibilities to explore.

Fashion Designer

I'm a fashion designer for a small design house in Los Angeles. It's not Calvin Klein, but it's a fun place to work and I love my job. Every day I have to find inspiration to create exciting and original outfits. It's challenging, but there is nothing more satisfying than seeing ideas come to life when someone actually wears my designs.

Before all the sewing, modeling, and photographing, someone has to come up with the original idea for an outfit. That may seem like a simple feat, but a designer must consider many things. For example, what will be the hot color three seasons from now? What is more important to women at the moment—glamour or comfort? What is today's fashionable skirt length? Fashion designers must be knowledgeable about clothing trends both past and present. A designer usually presents his or her ideas to employers through sketches, hence he or she must be able to draw well enough to make his or her concepts clear. The designer may drape fabrics on mannequins or models to get a feel for how they will look when sewn together.

Designers learn their craft by apprenticing with, or assisting a more established designer. Apprentices usually work for free. Then an apprentice moves up to assistant designer. Salaries for assistants can range from $15,000 to $30,000 a year. Full-fledged designers can make salaries from $30,000 to well into the millions for the most successful designers. That level of success comes through a combination of hard work, self-promotion, and luck.

Costume Designer

My great passion is going to the theater to watch plays. I enjoy making clothing, and I get straight A's in home economics. I even designed and sewed my entire wardrobe for school this year! When I heard my school was putting on a production of the musical Grease, *I offered to help out with the costumes, and they put me in charge after I showed them some clothes I had made. I found old leather jackets and letter sweaters at thrift stores, and I made poodle skirts*

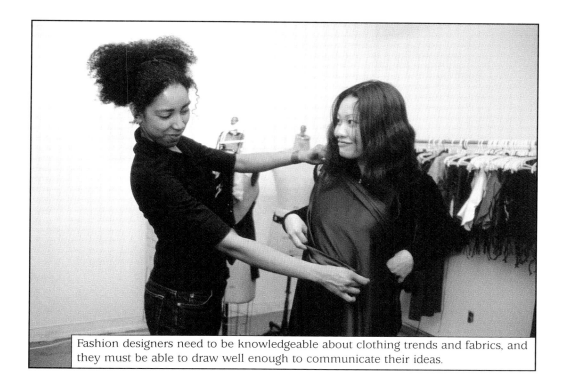

Fashion designers need to be knowledgeable about clothing trends and fabrics, and they must be able to draw well enough to communicate their ideas.

for the girls. It was exciting to be part of the show even though I was not performing. Watching the cast perform in clothes I created made me feel good, and I was happy to contribute to something that I am passionate about. Maybe I can design costumes for a living.

Some people do design costumes for a living. They work with directors of plays, operas, television shows, and films to create outfits for the performers. The designs must convey certain aspects of the story being told in the production. For example, a conservative suit would not work well for a character who is part of a street gang! If you are interested in this career, you may want to get involved with your high school drama

17

club. You can also offer to help get costumes together for small theater groups in your town. If you are hired for a paying position, expect to start low: $13,000 to $18,000 a year. Costume designers with skill and experience can make $40,000 or more in larger theater groups.

Dance, Exercise, or Sports Apparel Designer

I like to watch and participate in skiing, hockey, gymnastics, basketball, and just about any other competitive activity. I love the look of the uniforms with all those bright colors and slick designs. I try to imagine what kind of research must have gone into creating clothing for each sport. How do figure skating costumes allow for such freedom of movement? And how are football uniforms designed to be protective, yet flexible? The human body is capable of so many different kinds of movement. I want to study movement, and design the clothing that would help athletes perform their best.

Clothing designers interested in working with dance, exercise, and sports apparel are required to study human anatomy and textiles, or fabrics. Designers in this field may create items ranging from ballet shoes, to basketball shorts and jerseys, to spandex shorts and tops designed for working out at the gym. While dance and exercise wear designers generally work for large firms, they some-times open their own specialty stores. Designers of

Designers of dance, exercise or sporting apparel need to have an extensive knowledge of human anatomy.

athletic wear almost always work for larger manufacturers. There are many opportunities available in these fields, and competition for the jobs is not usually intense. Pay varies, depending on the size of the store or firm, and the skill and experience of the designer. Newcomers start in the low teens.

Bridal Gown Designer

I will never forget the way my sister looked in her beige satin wedding gown. Her dress seemed to sparkle and glow with all the joy she felt inside. It helped make the whole event so special. To this day I think wedding gowns are the most beautiful dresses in the entire world. When I saw a classified ad for a design job available at a store called Jennifer's Bridal Boutique, I practically ran there to show them my sketches. And believe it or not, my skills and enthusiasm got me the job. I could not be happier.

For many women, picking out the right wedding dress is an important decision. Because everyone has different taste in clothing, the bridal industry is flourishing. The designs of bridal gown designers must never be boring, but they must also never be outrageous or tasteless. It is important to read many bridal magazines, as well as mainstream fashion journals, since the definition of tasteless is always changing.

Bridal designers may work in small boutiques or in large department stores, and many have their

Superstar designer Vera Wang made a name for herself by designing bridal gowns.

own businesses. Salaries may range from $20,000 to $50,000 a year and beyond for the most successful and well-known designers.

Accessory Designer

When it comes to jewelry, Tonya is the most resourceful teenager I know! She does not have a lot of spending money, but she makes the most amazing things out of ordinary objects. Last month she gave me an incredible bracelet made out of paperclips and beads. She does such a good job, you would swear her jewelry is professionally made.

Jewelry is an important accessory. Shoes, glasses, scarves, hats, belts, ties, cufflinks, and gloves all fall into the accessory category. Each type of accessory requires special design skills. Unlike clothing designers, people who design jewelry almost always create the pieces themselves. They must have training and experience working with many materials before designing and creating jewelry to sell to customers. Paperclips and beads are a great place to start, but it is a long road up from there! Tonya may have a great future in jewelry design if she gets proper training and works hard to develop her skills. She could also become a jeweler. Besides designing, jewelers sell, repair, and appraise jewelry, which means they figure out how much money different pieces are worth.

Designing any kind of accessory requires artistic skill and usually some kind of special training. Shoe design is complicated, as it requires a thorough knowledge of the anatomy of feet. As with most design careers, accessory designers can work for large firms, department stores, small boutiques, or they may start their own businesses. They may earn as little as $10,000 a year or up into the millions, but the average salary is around $30,000 a year.

Fashion Photography

In high school, I took photos for the yearbook. I got to know lots of people because I photographed all the clubs and sports teams. I enjoyed it so much that I decided to pursue photography after graduation. A local newspaper hired me to photograph various events and personalities. It was great at first, but then I got bored; I wanted to do something more creative. I loved photographing people, but I wanted to be able to choose the settings and poses for my photos. A new, experimental fashion magazine was just starting up in my town, so I showed them some of my work. They gave me a freelance assignment photographing a line of clothing for a local designer. The pictures turned out well, and more assignments followed. I now have published work to show to larger

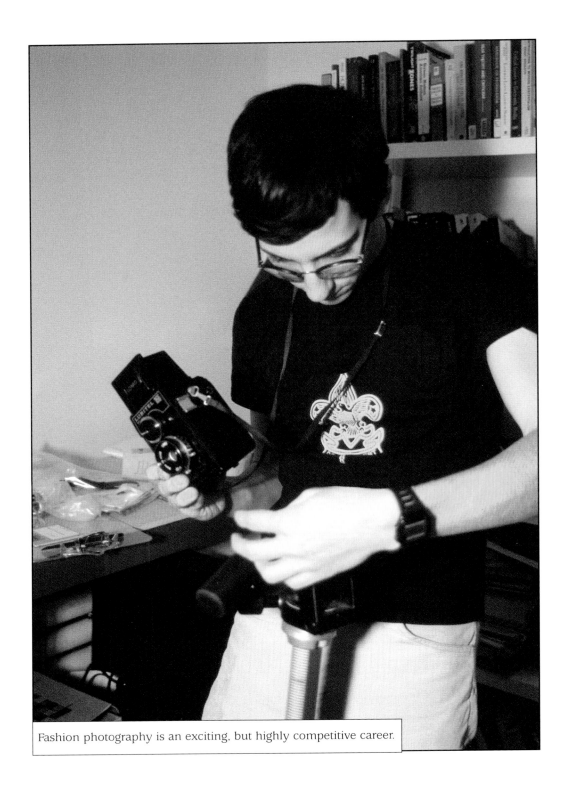

Fashion photography is an exciting, but highly competitive career.

magazines. Hopefully someday I will be able to leave the newspaper and photo-graph fashion full-time.

Photography is one of the most exciting and artistic careers available in the fashion world. It is also one of the most competitive. This is not a career for people looking for job security and a steady paycheck, though some well-established fashion photographers do have a constant work flow. Getting established is the difficult part, and it can involve many years of low pay and dry spells. For those willing to go the distance, fashion photography can be extremely rewarding. Photographers work freelance or full-time. Freelance pay depends on how much work you can find, and the success of the magazines you work for. Salaries range from zero (for internships) to millions for the most sought-after photographers. Average pay can be anywhere in between, generally from $20,000 to $60,000 a year.

Modeling

I'm on a jet to Paris, where I will be whisked off to a runway show. Then I will strut up and down the catwalk before flashing cameras, celebrities, and important fashion journalists. Then I'll be attending an incredible party, and I'll be interviewed for a television show.

Okay, that is actually the life I hope to have sometime soon. Right now I am being photographed for the Sears catalog and living with about eight other models in a cramped apartment in New York City. My manager has disappeared, and the runway show I was supposed to do next month was just canceled. And I'm too broke to pay the rent. Not very glamorous, but I am determined to make it in this career.

For some models, perseverance does lead to success. For others, it does not. Many people in the business suggest that newcomers have something else to fall back on. Modeling is one of the more unstable professions a person can choose, but it has many advantages, too. Successful models get to see the world and meet interesting people. There is also a chance to earn tremendous salaries. The connections one may make in modeling can be useful in landing other careers later on. The thrill of appearing in magazines and on television can be worth the work involved.

The main drawback is the lack of job security. However, many models complain of exhaustion. Posing in front of cameras all day can take a lot out of a person—physically and emotionally. Having the "right" look is essential. Otherwise, a model will have a difficult time finding work. But a young person with the right look and personality can do very well as a model.

Cosmetology

I am a high school student considering a career in fashion. I want to be close to the action, but I have no interest in modeling or photography. Last week when I went to have my hair done, I asked my stylist, Darlene, if she had any ideas. She told me about doing hair and wigs for important photo shoots. Darlene has worked with dozens of supermodels and many top-notch photographers. She is also a skilled makeup artist and has applied cosmetics for models in runway shows from Paris to Milan! Darlene also told me about manicuring, skin care, and salon management. I had no idea there were so many options!

The next time you look at a fashion magazine, consider the importance of cosmetology. How would all of those fabulous clothes look on models wearing poorly applied makeup and frizzy wigs? What if the models' fingernails were broken, and their eyebrows were crooked? Imagine a model with splotchy skin and pimples on the cover of *Vogue*! This is why cosmetology is a highly valued skill in the world of fashion. The workday for cosmetologists in salons tends to be more consistent than for those who work freelance.

Here are some brief descriptions of careers in this diverse field:

✔ **Makeup Artist**

Makeup artists work with designers and photographers to capture a certain look for the camera or runway. Many makeup artists work

Hairstylists and other cosmetologists play crucial roles in the world of fashion.

freelance. There are also job opportunities with salons, cosmetics companies, and even television and film studios.

✔ Hairdresser

Most of us are familiar with what a hairdresser does. Hairdressers cut and style hair freelance or for salons, department stores, or high fashion and theatrical events. They may also style wigs and hairpieces.

✔ Manicurist

Also known as a nail technician, this skilled worker cares for clients' hands and feet, or specifically, their fingernails and toenails. They use special tools and products to make fingernails and toenails look their best.

✔ Skin Care Specialist

These specialists, sometimes called estheticians, work at salons and cosmetics companies, where they help clients care for their skin. They must be knowledgeable and skilled in a variety of areas, ranging from skin care products, to massage, to treatments for skin disorders.

✔ Salon Manager

A manager of a hair salon may also be the owner. He or she is responsible for all operations, including everything from personnel to accounting to promotion. Salon managers usually do hair as well.

Window Display Design

Joseph had been working the cash register and folding sweaters at the Gap for a year. He was beginning to get bored, so he asked his manager for something more interesting to do. The manager suggested that Joe put together a window display.

He was thrilled! Joseph began gathering materials from art supply stores, like neon paint, Magic Markers, glitter, and stencils. He also found old fabric, furniture, and even a mirrored ball. He decided on a theme and created four window displays, each of which was distinct and eye-catching.

What pleased Joe's manager the most was that many customers were coming in to the store because they were drawn to the window displays. Joe took photos of his work so he could easily demonstrate his skills to larger department stores.

If you are looking for a career that utilizes your skills in both art and fashion, consider window display design. You can let your imagination run free, setting up props, painting backdrops, and posing mannequins. Window displays can tell an interesting story or simply convey a mood. Assistant window display designers (or trimmers) start at minimum wage and mainly assist the designer by moving things around and going out to pick up props. Assistants have more creative input as their relationship with the designer grows. Designers earn varying salaries, depending on where they work. A small retail store in Utah would not pay as high a salary as a store like Bloomingdale's or Macy's in New York City. Designers also have the option of freelancing, which requires that they pay for their own materials.

Tailor and Dressmaker

When I was little, my family did not have a lot of money. My father taught me to sew so that I could make my own clothes. We bought fabric, and my father drew up patterns. I would cut the fabric and sew the clothing together. It was fun to make an outfit, and it gave my father and me some special times together. By the time I reached high school, we were no longer poor, but I kept on sewing. It was such a challenge, and I made a lot of great things for my friends. I decided that tailoring was something I could do for a living that I would really enjoy. And I was already very good at it!

For someone who loves to sew, tailoring (working with men's clothing) or dressmaking (working with women's clothing) may be an excellent career choice. Tailors and dressmakers may work for small manufacturing firms, where they sew garments from start to finish. With larger

Tailoring or dressmaking are ideal careers for people who love to sew.

firms they usually specialize in sewing certain parts of a garment, like sleeves or lapels. Or they may be assigned to measuring, making patterns, or cutting fabric. Many tailors and dressmakers do alterations on garments that are already made. They can make an excellent living doing this—be it at a department store, at home, or by opening up a store. Besides sewing, these workers must accurately measure their clients' bodies so that clothing fits properly. Tailors and dressmakers can earn from $15,000 a year in the low range, to $60,000 a year on the high end.

The Business Side of Fashion

For those more suited to business than artistry, career possibilities in the fashion industry are plentiful. There are opportunities for terrific jobs in selling, buying, management, and marketing. These fashion careers tend to be more stable and secure than the creative occupations discussed in chapter 2.

Clothing and Fabric Sales

I love working with people! This is why I believe I would be a great salesperson. Since I enjoy fashion I have decided to look for a job selling clothing at a department store.

I think it sounds like fun to help others make decisions about what clothing looks right on them. I think I'd be really good at helping people decide what looks best on them. And I could suggest what accessories would look the

A retail clothing salesperson can advise customers on outfits and accessories while gaining valuable experience and knowledge of fashion.

best. It would be kind of like being a fashion consultant. And the more I sell, the more money I'd earn, so I would always be motivated to do my best.

Working in retail clothing or fabric sales can be an excellent career in itself, but it can also be a way to gain valuable experience in other fashion-related jobs. For example, by working in retail, a person working toward a career in clothing design could learn a great deal about how customers think, as well as what types of clothing sell better than others. Being surrounded by outfits all day long can also inspire ideas for new designs. And those who work in fabric (also called textile) sales can become familiar with the many different fabrics that exist. These people may also get a valuable store discount. Retail is a great springboard for positions such as store manager, buyer, sales representative, and window display designer.

Salespeople, whether working in clothing or textiles, should have the right type of personality for selling. They need to learn how to be outgoing without becoming obnoxious. They should be persuasive but not aggressive. It is a balancing act. Many people are born with this type of personality, but anyone can develop it with practice.

Clothing and fabric salespeople work on commission. This means that every time they sell an item, they get to keep a small percentage of the money made on the sale. Many people like working this way. It means that those who work hard are rewarded. Most salespeople also earn a small salary in addition to their commission (usually around minimum wage). Salespeople's hours tend to change from week to week, and generally include evening and weekend shifts.

We have all seen clothing salespeople at work, dealing with customers, folding sweaters, stocking shelves, or working a cash register. So how are a fabric salesperson's responsibilities different? The biggest difference is the product line. Textile sales requires learning a great deal of detailed information about fabrics. Textile salespeople must be able to convey that information to customers, who are generally designers and manufacturers.

Store Management

I did such a great job as a clothing salesperson with Pretty Plus that my supervisor decided to promote me to assistant manager. It is a great opportunity because I got a raise and I have more interesting responsibilities. Right now I just help the manager with his duties, but I hope that if I prove myself in this position, I will be promoted to manager, too. I am a very organized person. My past experience with customers has helped me to become persuasive, and I think I would be very good at supervising and motivating employees. I also feel that a job as manager would look excellent on my résumé in case I decide to pursue another career in fashion. But who knows, I may decide to stay in store management if I really like it.

Store managers do exactly what it sounds like they do: They manage an entire clothing store. Managers' responsibilities vary from store to store. They may deal with personnel, which involves hiring, firing, evaluating, and training new employees. They often work on special sales and inventory control, paperwork, customer disputes, and the supervision of salespeople. Sometimes these tasks are divided up among other managers—department managers, personnel managers, group managers, and operation managers. However, the store manager is in charge of all of the employees in the store, so he or she still needs to know what is happening in every department. Anyone going

Store managers are in charge of all the store's employees. They should be highly organized and able to handle pressure well.

into this position should be highly organized and should be able to handle pressure well.

Salaries for assistants may be low, but full-fledged managers usually earn around $50,000 a year. That figure can double or even triple with experience, especially in prestigious department stores in large cities.

Buying

As soon as I learned about buying, I knew it was the job for me. Just imagine, making a career out of shopping! Buying the right clothing for a department store can be tricky, not to mention exhausting. There are days when I come home feeling worn out. And most of what I do involves dealing with numbers, not fashion. I would not trade this job for anything. I

*get to travel, meet interesting people,
and go to great parties. And I get to
make use of my sense of style, decision-
making abilities, and accounting skills to
earn a terrific living.*

Did you ever wonder how all of the clothing hanging on racks at a store ends up there? Who picks it out, and how does he or she decide what to carry? These are the responsibilities of a buyer. Buyers need to have a good eye for quality and style because they are often expected to make quick and effective decisions. Buyers decide which items their store will be able to sell and how much of the item should be kept in stock. A buyer travels to the clothing vendor's showroom to examine garments, learn about what colors are available, and to discuss prices. If you are interested in buying as a career, you should be knowledgeable about the current fashion scene, the quality and construction of clothing, and different accounting methods. Most of the buyer's time is spent analyzing numbers and creating financial reports (reports that deal with money).

Buyers are generally well paid. Assistant buyers start between $18,000 and $30,000 a year, and those who are promoted to buyer can earn $25,000 to $80,00 a year, depending on the store.

Sales Representative

*I worked as a salesperson for a
department store in our local mall all
through high school. The job was okay,*

and it helped me save up for a car I wanted. But the salary I was making would not be enough to support me after I moved out of my parents' house. I was a good salesperson, but selling to the public got on my nerves. So when my career counselor suggested exploring a career as a sales representative, I was confused. My counselor then explained that sales representatives sell clothing, but not to the public. They work for manufacturers and try to sell merchandise to department store buyers. I would be able to use the selling skills I had acquired at the store, while making a better salary and avoiding customers! It sounded like an interesting option to explore.

Sales representatives are the people in the showrooms who assist the buyers in picking out garments. Sales representatives who work from home instead of at a showroom may have to travel to bring samples to the buyers. Reps must be able to answer any questions the buyers might have, so detailed knowledge of the product line is a must.

A sales rep should be a self-starter, someone who goes after a sale rather than waiting for one. Reps also need to possess personal style, flexibility (since hours are never nine to five), and good communication skills. Sales representatives work on commission, so how much they earn depends on how much they sell.

Image Consulting

"Darling, you look FABULOUS!"shouted Lucinda as she met up with her best friend, Louis, at their favorite nightclub. He was wearing a stylish, tailored suit and had just dyed his hair black. "The suit is perfection. Those lines are ideal for your body type because they show off your slim waist without making you look too skinny." Then Lucinda noticed his hair. "What is going on with that dye job?" she shrieked. "It's all wrong for your complexion!"

Louis smiled at his friend. She was decked out in a suitably festive, light green vintage dress. Her hair and make-up were perfect, as always. Just as he was about to defend his new hairstyle, a stranger interrupted. "Excuse me, but I overheard your critique of your friend's look. You've got a good eye!" The stranger pulled out a business card. "I work for an image consulting firm. We work with companies, athletes, celebrities, and wealthy clients to help them project the right image through fashion," he explained. "Would you like to come in for an interview?"

It has been said that some people naturally have fashion sense, while others do not. Often, people who live in the public eye need help picking out the right clothing, hairstyles, and

An image consultant must understand how colors work or do not work together.

cosmetics. This is how image consultants make their living.

A fashion consultant must have a knack for fashion, and he or she must also keep up-to-date on fashion trends. Fashion consultants must also understand the ways that specific colors do or do not work together. They need to figure out what type of silhouette works best for each client's body type. "Silhouette" is a fashion term that describes the outline of a piece of clothing.

Fashion consultants may work as freelancers or with a firm. The hours are not generally nine to five, since the schedule revolves around the client's needs. Those in the business say that the pay is excellent, since clients are willing to spend a lot of money to look good. The difficult part is actually finding and holding on to the clients.

Production Assistant

I never wanted to be a fashion designer. I do like to sew, and I am fascinated by the way clothing and accessories are put together. But I am a very organized, business-oriented person. While working as a retail salesperson in Chicago, I read the classified ads daily. I was trying to find an office job that would incorporate my interest and background in clothing. I was lucky. There was an opening for a production assistant with a small design firm, so I asked my boss what a production assistant does. She explained that the main responsibilities are supervising collections in all stages of development—from the initial idea to fabrication. This includes things like ordering materials, assembling the garments or accessories, and overseeing shipments from manufacturers to warehouses. It sounded perfect for me.

Production assistants have very hectic, but rewarding careers. They make sure that the manufacturing and shipping of a design company's clothing goes smoothly. Another aspect of the job is ordering fabrics and materials from different companies and assuring that they are shipped to the clothing manufacturers. The production assistant is also involved in drawing up the line list, which is a detailed description of items that are available from the design company. Sometimes stores order from the line list rather than going through the buyer and sales representative. Finally, the production assistant must be sure that finished clothing ships from the manufacturer to the warehouse (the building where the company's clothing is stored).

A production assistant must be highly organized, skilled with numbers, and work well with people. Sewing, computer, and typing skills are also helpful. Pay may start low, but top-rated design firms will pay top dollar for a skillful and experienced production assistant they can rely on.

Preparing for a Career in Fashion

If you have checked out the fashion industry and feel that it might be a good career choice for you, you may be wondering what types of special schooling and fancy degrees you will need in order to go after these jobs. Some jobs in fashion do not necessarily require a degree or special schooling, as long as you have the natural talent and instinct that it takes. Other careers, like cosmetology, are impossible to get into without some special classes. In either case there are many things you can do to increase your chances of landing that first job.

Sewing and Design Careers

No college degree is necessary for entry into these fields. But for jobs that involve designing clothing or accessories, it is important that you are able to draw in order to get your ideas across. Try to take as many drawing and art classes in school that you can. It is also a good idea to study art history. Many designers are inspired by different kinds of art, like painting and sculpture.

Studying art and art history is a good idea for an aspiring designer.

Sewing, home economics, and computer literacy are classes to take for a future in design. And to have a good sense of what is currently happening in the world of fashion, read as many fashion magazines as possible. Looking at other people's designs will help you define your own style.

If you do have the opportunity to go to fashion school, it can give you an edge over those entering the business with no training. And certain design jobs, like shoe, hat, and jewelry design, are impossible to perform without some specialized training. You can find the names and addresses of some important fashion schools in the For More Information section at the back of this book. These schools are usually located in fashion centers like New York City, Los Angeles, and Miami. There are also some great schools outside of the United States. Canada has the reputable Montreal Superior Fashion School, Ryerson Polytechnic Institute in Toronto, and George Brown Community College in Toronto. The programs at fashion schools are specifically designed to teach you all you will need to know to succeed in a design career.

For sewing jobs like being a seamstress or a tailor, no drawing skills are required. Taking sewing and home economics in high school is a good idea, and tailoring and pattern-making classes would also be helpful. There are even correspondence courses (classes you take at home, through the mail or over the Internet) for sewing, tailoring, and pattern making.

Photography

Many people in the industry say it is necessary to have a college degree in photojournalism in order to make it in fashion photography. However, some photographers simply have a "good eye," or a natural knack for taking a great photo. Legendary photographer Richard Avedon learned how to take photos in the merchant marine, and the well-respected Bill Cunningham started out as a writer.

Budding photographers can develop a style and hone their skills by buying a camera, experimenting, and practicing. Many high schools offer photography classes, and working for the school newspaper and yearbook can be a valuable experience to prepare you for a career in photography. Most colleges have a photography department and many offer it as a major.

Modeling

Success in modeling has more to do with having the ideal look than receiving any kind of training. Models do need to know how to pose and work a runway, but this can be learned by studying fashion magazines and watching fashion shows on television. Attending modeling classes can help someone develop his or her potential, but anyone considering a school should check its credentials very carefully.

Cosmetology

Jobs in cosmetology involve specialized skills and require specific training and licensing. The good news is that the training you need is easy to get. If you attend a public high school, you may have access to a vocational school. Often when you reach tenth grade you can split your day between your normal high school classes and the cosmetology classes at a vocational school. These classes are usually free. Check with your high school to see if your state offers these special schools. If not, cosmetology school can cost anywhere from $2,000 to $7,000 a year, and you can pay over a period of time.

Once you have received training, you need to apply for a cosmetology license. This involves taking a test to show how much you learned in your classes. Check with your high school or cosmetology school to find out more about getting licensed in your state or province.

Business Careers

There is no specialized training required for business jobs in the fashion industry. College can give you an edge over the competition but is not necessary. Most of what you learn for these careers comes from starting at the bottom of the ladder, watching, listening, and learning. If you do decide on college, business and accounting courses would be helpful. Learning how to type, use computers, and communicate well with others will also give you an advantage in the marketplace.

Finding Your
First Job

Finding your first job in fashion can be a daunting task. You should not be discouraged if you have to start out as someone's assistant, an intern, or as a low-paid cashier. Some of the most successful people in the industry started out the very same way. Here are some tips to help you get started.

The Résumé

Your résumé is an advertisement for you. A résumé is a sheet of paper that shows your skills, your experience, and your plans for the future. You send an employer a résumé, by mail or fax, after finding out about a job opening. Check with your school's career center or guidance counselor for examples of how résumés should be set up.

The résumé is the first impression you make on an employer, so it should look good. A neatly typed, mistake-free, and well-designed résumé printed on quality paper shows an employer in the fashion industry that you care about detail and appearances. Be creative when putting the résumé together, but try not to make the design too flashy or distracting.

Since this may be your first job, the "experience" section of your résumé may be a little thin. Do not be afraid to include information like work on your school newspaper or yearbook, sewing classes, or theater experience. Mention anything you have done that might pertain to the job you are seeking. Include sample photographs or sketches with your résumé only if they are requested by the employer.

If you are mailing your résumé to a company, you should include a cover letter addressed to a specific person. It needs to look just as neat as the résumé and should be typed on good paper. The cover letter should include your address and phone number, and should state which position you are seeking. Good things to describe are your skills, experience, and the reasons why you think you would be valuable to the company. Always thank the employer for his or her time, and always sign the letter by hand.

The Portfolio

Some fashion jobs require that you put together a portfolio. The portfolio is a book you assemble that displays your work. It may include fashion sketches you have drawn, photographs you have taken or posed for, window displays you have designed, or pictures of faces you have made up.

A portfolio, a book you assemble with samples of your work, is a must for many jobs in the fashion industry.

If your résumé is the advertisement, these are the delicious samples!

You can buy an empty portfolio at an art supply store. It does not need to cost a fortune, but should be attractive and clean. Your portfolio should include between ten and twelve examples of your best, most eye-catching work. Keep it up-to-date, and try to show a wide range of sketches or photos. Finally, this book should be with you at all times. You never know when a surprising opportunity will come up.

The Interview

After your résumé, cover letter, and portfolio are prepared, there are many things you can do to get ready for the interview. First, what do you need to know about yourself? You should be aware of your strengths and weaknesses. That way, during the interview you can concentrate on downplaying your weaknesses, and emphasizing your strengths. Knowing things about the company you are applying to is a little less complicated. You can research the company's products or services using the Internet, your school's counseling or career center, or your public library. The facts and information that you learn are sure to impress the interviewer.

When you do go to the interview, make sure you arrive on time. It is also very important to look good. A fashion employer will expect you to possess good personal style and to pay close attention to personal grooming. Make sure your hair is neatly styled and that your fingernails are

First impressions are important in the fashion world, so pay close attention to personal grooming when you go to a job interview.

clean, and try not to wear heavy makeup or flashy outfits.

First impressions are important in the fashion world. Use this book not only to start figuring out what part of the fashion industry is best for you but also to help you understand what it will take to get there. Anyone can do it if he or she wants it badly enough. With passion, determination, discipline, and a positive outlook, you can go anywhere you want in the fashion world!

Glossary

accessory Small article of clothing, like a shoe, belt, or piece of jewelry.

appraise To determine the worth of a valuable.

buyer Person who purchases clothing from a manufacturer for a store.

commission Percentage of a salesperson's profits that he or she is entitled to keep.

cosmetology Also known as "beauty careers," includes hairdressing, manicuring, and skin care.

esthetician Skin care specialist.

fashion consultant One who professionally advises others on their image and assists their fashion choices.

fashion designer One who comes up with the original idea and design for an outfit.

garment   Article of clothing.

line list   List of clothing items created by a production assistant for use by a store in ordering clothing.

personnel   Department of a clothing store or salon responsible for hiring, firing, and evaluating employees.

showroom   Room where a vendor shows clothing to a buyer.

silhouette   Outline of a piece of clothing.

spandex   Highly flexible fabric used to design clothing for athletes and dancers.

trimmer   Assistant window display designer.

WᴀW

For More
Information

In the United States

Amalgamated Clothing and Textile
    Workers Union
15 Union Square West
New York, NY 10003
(212) 242-0700

American Apparel Manufacturers Association
2500 Wilson Boulevard, Suite 301
Arlington, VA 22201
Toll free: (800) 520-2262
http://www.americanapparel.org

Bureau of Wholesale Sales Representatives
1100 Spring Street NW, Suite 700
Atlanta, GA 30309
Toll free: (800) 877-1808
http://www.bwsr.com

Clothing Manufacturers Association
    of the USA
1290 Avenue of the Americas
Suite 1061
New York, NY 10104

Fashion Group International, Inc.
597 Fifth Avenue, 8th Floor
New York, NY 10017
(212) 593-1715
http://www.fgi.org

Fashion Institute of Technology
27th Street & 7th Avenue
New York, NY 10001
(212) 217-7999
http://www.fitnyc.suny.edu

International Association of
    Clothing Designers
475 Park Avenue South, 17th Floor
New York, NY 10016
(212) 685-6602

National Beauty Career Center
3839 White Plains Road
Bronx, NY 19467
(718) 330-1280

Parsons School of Design
66 Fifth Avenue
New York, NY 10011
Toll free: (800) 252-0852
http://www.parsons.edu

Professional Photographers of America
229 Peachtree Street NE, Suite 2200
Atlanta, GA 30303
Toll free: (800) 786-6277
http://www.ppa-world.org

United Garment Workers of America
4207 Lebanon Road
Hermitage, TN 37076
(615) 889-9221

In Canada

Canada Apparel Federation
130 Slater Street, Suite 1050
Ottawa, ON K1P 6E2
(613) 231-3220
http://www.apparel.ca

Flare
(Canadian fashion magazine)
(416) 596-5000
http://www.flare.com

Manitoba Fashion Institute Training Center
365 Bannatyne Avenue, 3rd Floor
Winnipeg, MB R3A 0E5
(204) 942-7314
http://www.apparel-manitoba.org

School of Fashion and Creative Technologies
George Brown College
P.O. Box 1015, Station B
Toronto, ON M5T 2T9
(416) 415-2000
Toll free: (800) 265-2002
http:www.gbrownc.on.ca

School of Fashion at Ryerson Polytechnic
    University
350 Victoria Street
Toronto, ON M5B 2K3
(416) 979-5000
http://www.ryerson.ca
e-mail:prosstod@acs.ryerson.ca

Toronto Fashion Incubator
325 Adelaide Street West
Toronto, ON M5V 1P9
(416) 971-7117
http://www.fashionincubator.on.ca

WⱥW

For Further Reading

Beckett, Kathleen. *Careers Without College: Fashion.* Princeton, NJ: Peterson's, 1992.

Black, Judy. *Now Hiring: Fashion.* New York: Crestwood House, 1994.

Dignan, Renee, ed. *Singer Sewing Reference Library: Tailoring.* Minnetonka, MN: Cy DeCosse Incorporated, 1988.

Dolber, Roslyn. *Opportunities in Fashion Careers.* Lincolnwood, IL: NTC Publishing Group, 1993.

Hewitt, Sally. *The Clothes We Wear.* Austin, TX: Raintree Steck-Vaughn, 1997.

Mauro, Lucia. *Careers for Fashion Plates & Other Trendsetters.* Lincolnwood, IL: NTC Publishing Group, 1996.

———. *VGM's Career Portraits: Fashion.* Lincolnwood, IL: NTC Publishing Group, 1996.

Index

About the Author
John Giacobello is a freelance journalist and a musician. His first CD came out in spring 2000.

Photo Credits
Cover by Shalhevet Moshe. All interior shots by Shalhevet Moshe except p. 8 © Corbis International; p. 11 © Archive Photos; p. 21 © Sean Roberts/Everett Collection; p. 28 by Ira Fox; and p. 32 © David Fleurant/Uniphoto.

Layout
Geri Giordano